CIVIL WAR
HIGHLIGHTS

POLITICS
OF THE WAR

1861–1865

TIM COOKE

A+

Smart Apple Media

This edition published in 2013 by

Smart Apple Media, an imprint of Black Rabbit Books

PO Box 3263, Mankato, MN 56002

www.blackrabbitbooks.com

Brown Bear Books Ltd.

Editorial Director: Lindsey Lowe
Managing Editor: Tim Cooke
Children's Publisher: Anne O'Daly
Picture Manager: Sophie Mortimer
Creative Director: Jeni Child

Library of Congress Cataloging-in-Publication Data
Politics of the war : 1861-1865 / edited by Tim Cooke.
    p. cm. -- (Civil War highlights)
 Includes bibliographical references and index.
 Summary: "In an alphabetical almanac format, describes the
various actions taken in the Union and in the Confederacy to
support the war effort. It explains the relative strengths of the
two economies. It also examines the war's lasting impact on
American politics"--Provided by publisher.
 ISBN 978-1-59920-818-3 (library binding)
1. United States--Politics and government--1861-1865--Juve-
nile literature. 2. Confederate States of America--Politics and
government. 3. United States--History--Civil War, 1861-1865--
Influence. I. Cooke, Tim, 1961-
 E468.P655 2012
 973.7--dc23
                                    2012001309

Printed in the United States of America at Corporate
Graphics, North Mankato, Minnesota

PO1437

2-2012

9 8 7 6 5 4 3 2 1

Picture Credits

Front Cover: Library of Congress

Corbis: 9, 31, 32, 34; Bettmann 24, 30, 33; **Library
of Congress:** 4, 6, 8, 10, 11, 12, 13, 14, 16, 17, 18,
22, 25, 26, 27, 28, 29, 35, 36, 37, 38, 40, 41, 42, 43;
National Archives of America: 7, 15, 19, 20, 21, 23,
39; **Shutterstock:** Doug Ellis 5

All Artworks: Windmill Books.

Contents

Introduction

While the fighting went on, politics in the North continued much as normal. The Republicans and the Democrats vied for power. In the South, on the other hand, political parties were banned.

At the heart of the Civil War was a political question: what should happen about slavery? When war began, however, few politicians mentioned slavery. In the North, President Abraham Lincoln said that he was fighting to hold together the Union. In the South, Confederate politicians said that the war was necessary to uphold the rights of the states.

Lincoln came from the new Republican Party, which opposed any spread of slavery. The party was barely seven years old when the Civil War began. Thanks partly to the North's victory in the war, it would dominate U.S. politics for some 70 years. Lincoln managed to gather people with a range of political opinions and get them to work together for the Union cause.

Confederate Vice President Alexander H. Stephens spent much of the war criticizing President Jefferson Davis.

IN THIS TEMPLE
AS IN THE HEARTS OF THE PEOPLE
FOR WHOM HE SAVED THE UNION
THE MEMORY OF ABRAHAM LINCOLN
IS ENSHRINED FOREVER

The Lincoln Memorial in Washington, D.C., was built in the early 20th century to commemorate the president who saved the Union.

In the South, meanwhile, the Confederate President Jefferson Davis faced a more challenging task. The Confederacy was founded on the idea of states' rights, and many Southern politicians disliked the idea of a national government. In order to make the most of the South's relatively scarce resources, the government also introduced many unpopular measures.

In this book

Politics of the War describes the various actions taken in the Union and in the Confederacy to support the war effort. It explains the relative strengths of the two economies. It also examines the war's lasting impact on American politics. A timeline that runs across the bottom of the pages throughout the book traces the course of the war on the battlefield and other developments in North America and the rest of the world. At the back of the book is a Need to Know feature, which will help you relate subjects to your studies at school.

Democratic Party

The Democratic Party played a pivotal role in the lead-up to the Civil War. In the South, there were no political parties during the war, but the Democrats continued their opposition in the North.

THE GREAT MATCH AT BALTIMORE,
BETWEEN THE "ILLINOIS BANTAM", AND THE "OLD COCK" OF THE WHITE HOUSE.

This 1860 cartoon pokes funs at the fighting among the Democrats. It shows Stephen A. Douglas as a fighting cock who has defeated President James Buchanan for the party's presidential nomination.

Since the 1830s, the Democratic Party had emerged as one of the two major U.S. political parties. Its specific policies varied between states, but they all reflected a common belief in the need to limit federal government's control over the nation.

1861 January–March

CIVIL WAR

JANUARY 2, SOUTH CAROLINA Fort Johnson in Charleston Harbor is occupied by Confederate troops.

JANUARY 5, ALABAMA Alabama troops seize forts Morgan and Gaines, giving Confederate forces control of Mobile Bay.

JANUARY 9, MISSISSIPPI Leaders vote to leave the Union. Mississippi is the second state to join the Confederacy.

JANUARY 10, FLORIDA Florida leaves the Union.

JANUARY 11, ALABAMA Alabama leaves the Union.

OTHER EVENTS

JANUARY 15, UNITED STATES Engineer Elisha Otis invents the safety elevator.

JANUARY 29, UNITED STATES Kansas joins the Union as the 34th state.

January

Political changes

In the 1850s, the question of slavery brought great political changes. A Democratic senator from Illinois, Stephen Douglas, introduced the Kansas–Nebraska Act in 1854, which allowed slavery in the new western states. Northern opponents of slavery were so outraged they formed a new party, the Republican Party.

Before the end of the decade, the Republicans had become the majority party in the North. In the South, the Democrats continued to dominate. During the presidency of Democrat James Buchanan (1857–1861), however, Southern and Northern Democrats split over the issue of slavery. The split was confirmed during their national convention of 1860.

Abraham Lincoln, the Republican candidate in the 1860 presidential election, benefited from the Democrats' in-fighting. He won despite having no support in the South. His election would bring about the secession crisis, and then the Civil War. In the South, Jefferson Davis, a former Democratic senator from Mississippi, was elected president of the newly formed Confederate States of America.

President Abraham Lincoln, realizing the need to establish loyalty from his political opponents, was quick to appoint Democrats to his cabinet. Four members of his original seven-man cabinet were Democrats, including Secretary of War Simon Cameron, Treasury Secretary Salmon P. Chase, Navy Secretary Gideon Welles, and Postmaster General Montgomery Blair.

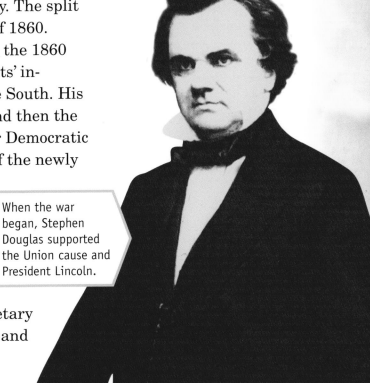

When the war began, Stephen Douglas supported the Union cause and President Lincoln.

JANUARY 19, GEORGIA
Georgia votes to leave the Union.

JANUARY 26, LOUISIANA
Louisiana becomes the sixth state to leave the Union.

FEBRUARY 4, ALABAMA
Leaders from the South meet in the state capital, Montgomery. They choose Jefferson Davis of Mississippi as their president and write a constitution for the Confederate States of America.

FEBRUARY 7, ALABAMA/MISSISSIPPI
The Choctaw Indian Nation forms an alliance with the South. Other Indian tribes follow later.

FEBRUARY, UNITED STATES
The first moving picture system is patented.

MARCH, RUSSIA
Czar Alexander II abolishes serfdom (a form of slavery).

February   March

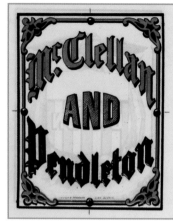  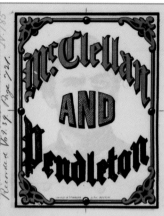 

A ribbon from the 1864 presidential campaign of Democrat George B. McClellan.

Democrats in wartime

The Northern Democratic Party remained divided. The larger group was described as War Democrats. They supported Lincoln's efforts to keep the Union together by force and to win the war against secession. Despite opposition from his own party, Lincoln followed appointing Democrats to his cabinet by appointing more Democrats to the Union Army. He commissioned Benjamin F. Butler, Nathaniel P. Banks, and John A. McClernand as senior Union generals.

The smaller Democratic group in the North were called the Peace Democrats; they were also known as "Copperheads," after a poisonous snake. These Democrats opposed Lincoln and the war effort, arguing that the Union should make peace with the Confederacy. Prominent Copperheads included New York Governor Horatio Seymour and Ohio Congressman Clement Vallandigham. Lincoln was tough on the Copperheads, whom

1861
April–June

CIVIL WAR

APRIL 12, SOUTH CAROLINA Confederates fire on Fort Sumter in Charleston Harbor in the first shots of the Civil War.

APRIL 15, THE NORTH President Lincoln calls for 75,000 recruits across the North to fight the South.

APRIL 19, WASHINGTON, D.C. President Lincoln declares a naval blockade of Southern states.

APRIL 19, BALTIMORE Mayor George Brown bans Union troops from the city after they are attacked by an angry pro-Confederate mob.

OTHER EVENTS

APRIL, EGYPT A search party sets out from Cairo to find the explorers John Speke and James Grant, who have gone missing while looking for the source of the Nile River.

April

he accused of helping the South. Lincoln had Vallandigham arrested and tried in military court. Found guilty of obstructing the war effort, he was exiled to the Confederacy.

The 1864 election

Although they were divided, Lincoln still saw the Democrats as a threat. As the presidential election of 1864 approached, he worried that the Democrats might win and make peace with the South. There was good reason for his fears. In the 1862 Congressional elections, the Democrats had shown they were again a force to be reckoned with. They won 77 seats in the House of Representatives to the Republicans' 103.

In 1864, the Democrats chose as their presidential candidate George B. McClellan, a popular general who had been sacked by Lincoln. To counter this, Lincoln chose a War Democrat from the South, Andrew Johnson of Tennessee, as his vice-presidential running mate. In the event, Lincoln was lucky. Union armies won some key victories in the run-up to the November election, and he was reelected by a landslide.

After the war, the Democrats and the Republicans became the two major parties in a two-party system. They remain the major parties today.

Here the Peace Democrats are shown as the deadly Copperhead snakes.

PEACE DEMOCRATS

The Peace Democrats were given their "Copperheads" nickname by the *New York Tribune* newspaper, which compared them to a poisonous snake. By 1863, the name was commonly used. The Copperheads criticized Lincoln's policies, such as conscription, the arrest and imprisonment of political opponents, and the Emancipation Proclamation, which made any compromise with the Confederacy impossible. Copperhead feeling was strongest in the border states, especially where slavery continued. Farmers feared their way of life would be ended by capitalists from the Northeast.

APRIL 23, VIRGINIA Major General Robert E. Lee becomes commander of land and naval forces in Virginia.

APRIL 27, WASHINGTON, D.C. Abraham Lincoln suspends "habeus corpus," a law that protects individuals from being arrested for little reason.

MAY 9, GREAT BRITAIN Britain announces it will remain neutral in the Civil War.

MAY 20, NORTH CAROLINA North Carolina is the last state to leave the Union.

JUNE 20, VIRGINIA West Virginia is unhappy at Virginia's decision to leave the Union. It breaks from the Confederacy and is admitted into the Union.

APRIL, AUSTRALIA Robert Burke and William Wills, who led the first expedition across Australia, narrowly miss a rendezvous with their colleagues; Burke and Wills will die in the Outback.

JUNE, UNITED STATES "Aeronaut" Thaddeus Lowe demonstrates his hot-air balloon for President Abraham Lincoln.

May   June

Economy of the Confederacy

Before the start of the Civil War, a small number of Southerners grew rich from using slaves to grow cotton, tobacco, and sugar. Their wealth underpinned the whole Southern economy.

Union soldiers steal Southern cattle in a raid. The South's agriculture was badly damaged in the war.

The South appeared wealthy between 1800 and 1860, but its economy was fragile. It depended on a few cash crops, slave labor, and some underdeveloped industry and manufacturing. The Civil War exposed the fragility of the South's economy.

1861
July–September

CIVIL WAR

JULY 2, WISCONSIN Union forces push back Confederates near Hainesville in the Battle of Hoke's Run.

JULY 6, CUBA The Confederate raiding ship CSS *Sumter* captures seven Union vessels in Cuban waters.

JULY 21, VIRGINIA The first major battle of the war is fought at Manassas/First Bull Run. Confederates led by Pierre G.T. Beauregard defeat General Irvin McDowell's larger Union army.

OTHER EVENTS

JULY, UNITED STATES The Pony Express arrives in San Francisco, beginning a cross-contry mail service.

JULY, UNITED STATES Congress approves the printing of the first dollar bills, known as "greenbacks."

July

Plantation system

The plantation system of slave-based farming became established in the South in the 1700s. Its popularity grew, however, in the 1800s. Factories were built in Britain and the northeastern United States for weaving cloth. They created a huge demand for Southern-grown cotton.

This was the period when Alabama, Mississippi, Louisiana, and, later, Texas were settled and joined the Union. The warm climate and rich soil of the Deep South were ideal for growing cotton, and white planters moved to the new states with their slaves to establish cotton plantations.

Slavery was also used to grow other cash crops, such as tobacco, rice, sugar, and hemp. But the profit from cotton-growing was so high that in time many planters used all their land and slaves to grow cotton. This meant they had to buy corn and meat from smaller local farms. Even nonslaveholders in the South became dependent on the planters for some of their income.

This label from a cigar box shows an idealized view of slave life on a Southern tobacco plantation.

Dominance of cotton

By 1861, cotton from the South accounted for three-quarters of the world supply. Southerners declared that "Cotton is king." Observers in the North noted, however, that the Southern economy lacked diversity. In 1860, almost 90 percent of U.S. manufacturing capacity and two-thirds of its railroad tracks

AUGUST 10, MISSOURI
The Battle of Wilson's Creek is the first major battle on the Mississippi River; it sees the first death of a Union general, Nathaniel Lyon.

SEPTEMBER 3, KENTUCKY
Confederate forces invade Kentucky, ending its neutrality.

SEPTEMBER 12–15, WEST VIRGINIA
General Robert E. Lee's Confederate forces are beaten at the Battle of Cheat Mountain Summit.

SEPTEMBER 19, KENTUCKY
The Battle of Barbourville sees Confederates raid an empty Union guerrilla training base.

AUGUST, UNITED STATES
The U.S. Government introduces the first income tax to raise funds for the war.

August   **September**

Slaves work a cotton gin. The invention of the gin speeded up the production of cotton in the pre-war South.

SOUTHERN TECHNOLOGY

The invention of the cotton gin in 1793 led to a boom in productivity for the South's cotton industry. The gin made it possible to separate cotton seeds quickly and efficiently from the cotton fiber. Previously, the job had to be done by hand and was much slower.

were in the North. The Confederacy had only one factory that could cast large cannons, the Tredegar Iron Works in Richmond, Virginia.

Cotton blockade

At the start of war, the South made an error. Confederate President Jefferson Davis encouraged planters not to sell cotton to Britain and Europe. He hoped the Europeans would be so desperate to get cotton that they would force the North to stop the war. But Britain had already developed sources of cotton from Egypt and India, so its textile production continued. The South's economy was badly damaged as cotton piled up in warehouses.

When the Confederate government reversed its policy of withholding cotton from Britain in 1863, it was too late. By that time the Union blockade of the Southern coastline had effectively strangled Southern trade.

Paying for the war

Before the war, people in the South had paid few taxes. The Confederacy was built on an opposition to central government. But as the cost of the war grew, the Confederate government tried to introduce two taxes in 1861. It did not have very much

1861 October–December

CIVIL WAR

OCTOBER 21, KENTUCKY 7,000 Union troops defeat Confederates at the Battle of Camp Wildcat on Wildcat Mountain.

OCTOBER 21, MISSOURI Union attempts to cross the Potomac River at Harrison's Island fail in the Battle of Ball's Bluff.

OCTOBER 21, MISSOURI The Union controls southeastern Missouri after the Battle of Fredericktown.

NOVEMBER 7, MISSOURI Ulysses S. Grant's Union forces defeat Confederates at the Battle of Belmont.

OTHER EVENTS

OCTOBER 22, UNITED STATES The first telegraph line is completed linking the east and west coasts.

NOVEMBER 1, CONFEDERACY Jefferson Davis is elected as president of the Confederacy.

October   November

success. Individual states were responsible for collecting taxes, but many were reluctant to do so. The Confederacy only raised between 5 and 6 percent of its war funds by taxation, compared with the Union's 21 percent.

The Confederacy raised a further $34 million by promising lenders a good price on cotton after the war. But its main source of income came from printing paper money. The Confederacy printed $1.5 billion in bank notes during the war. This led to inflation that neared 9,000 percent by the end of the conflict.

Hard times

By 1863 life in the South was hard. There were shortages of even basic foods such as sugar, flour, and salt. War had destroyed much of the Southern farmland, and the army took much of the limited food supplies. Slaves also left the fields in thousands to join invading Union soldiers. In fall 1864 a Union army marched through Georgia, destroying everything it could not eat: fields, houses, cotton, gins, and railroads.

Remarkably, given the devastation of much of the Confederacy during the conflict, the South's economy recovered within a decade. By 1871 the South was exporting more cotton than it had before the war started.

Richmond, Virginia, was the capital of the Confederacy. It was home to vital iron works that supplied cannons.

SOUTHERN TOWNS

The prewar South had some towns and cities, but they were all relatively small. In 1860, only 7 percent of Southerners lived in towns of more than 2,500 people. The largest city, New Orleans, had a population of 170,000. Although it was nearly four times bigger than the next-largest Southern city, Charleston, South Carolina, it was much smaller than Northern cities. At the start of the war, for example, New York's population stood at more than a million. The Southern towns existed to support the agricultural economy. They were home to mills, gins, and agricultural supply stores, as well as storage yards to keep goods before they were shipped.

NOVEMBER 8, CUBA
The British steamer *Trent* is stopped by Union warship *San Jacinto* in an action that breaks international law, as Britain is not a combatant in the Civil War.

NOVEMBER 8, KENTUCKY
The Battle of Ivy Mountain, also known as Ivy Creek, sees Union soldiers push Confederates back into Virginia.

DECEMBER 20, VIRGINIA Union troops defeat Confederate cavalry under J.E.B. "Jeb" Stuart in the Battle of Dranesville.

NOVEMBER 19, UNITED STATES
Julia Howe writes the first verses of "The Battle Hymn of the Republic."

DECEMBER 14, GREAT BRITAIN Prince Albert, the husband of Queen Victoria, dies, plunging his wife into a long period of mourning.

Economy of the Union

The North was much better placed than the South to finance the war and to keep its army supplied. Its industrial and diverse economy was based on the manufacture of consumer goods.

An iron works in New York. The North had 110,000 factories in 1860, compared to 18,000 in the South.

On the eve of war, Union general William T. Sherman wrote to a Southern friend, "You are rushing into war with one of the most powerful, ingeniously mechanical, and determined people on earth—right at your doors. You are bound to fail."

1862 January–March

CIVIL WAR

JANUARY 18 ARIZONA
The Confederate Territory of Arizona is formed from part of what was the old Territory of New Mexico.

FEBRUARY 6, TENNESSEE
Union General Ulysses S. Grant takes the Confederate Fort Henry. The Tennessee River is now under Union control as far as Alabama.

FEBRUARY 16, TENNESSEE
Grant's troops take Fort Donelson; 15,000 Southerners surrender.

OTHER EVENTS

FEBRUARY, UNITED STATES
"The Battle Hymn of the Republic" is published. It quickly becomes a popular marching song in the Union.

January   February

An economic powerhouse

Sherman was right. The Northern states had a massive economic advantage over the South. With a population of 22 million, twice that of the South's, the North produced virtually all of the country's iron, coal, and firearms. It also controlled nearly all of the country's merchant ships and railroads, as well as 75 percent of the country's farmland. Northerners held three-quarters of the nation's total taxable wealth.

While such advantages gave the North a stable base from which to fight the war, however, they did not add up to military power. The North needed the efforts of politicians, financiers, and businessmen to harness factories, trains, and wheatfields for the war effort. And the war effort also had to be paid for.

A fiscal-military revolution

By New Year's Day 1862 the Union government had run out of money. To solve the crisis a group of businessmen, bankers, and attorneys put forward a plan to Congress and Salmon P. Chase, the Secretary of the Treasury. They proposed paying for the war by using a mixture of loans, issuing paper money, and raising taxes.

The plan resulted in the Legal Tender Act of February 1862. The act allowed the government to issue $150 million in Treasury

A port in California. The government encouraged the building of a railroad to the Pacific coast.

FEBRUARY 25, TENNESSEE With the loss of forts Henry and Donelson, Nashville is the first Confederate state capital to fall to Union forces.

MARCH 6–8, ARKANSAS The Confederates are defeated at the Battle of Pea Ridge, the largest battle on Arkansas soil.

MARCH 8–9, VIRGINIA The Battle of Hampton Roads sees Confederate and Union ironclads fight to a standstill.

MARCH 17, VIRGINIA The Union Army of the Potomac sails to Fort Monroe to begin the Peninsular Campaign.

MARCH, EAST AFRICA Zanzibar becomes an independent nation.

MARCH 10, UNITED STATES The first U.S. paper money goes into circulation.

SPLIT ECONOMIES

It was the difference between how the North and South made money—their economies—that lay at the heart of the political conflict that led to war. The Northern states based their economy on manufacturing. They built up modern infrastructure to support entrepreneurship and business. When possible, goods were built in the Northern states and little was imported. In the South, things were very different. Its economy was based on agriculture, largely cash crops to sell abroad. The South had to buy manufactured goods from the North or abroad. Plantation owners relied on slaves to increase the huge profits they made from cotton.

notes, known as greenbacks. It was compulsory to accept the notes for all public or private debts, with just two exceptions: customs duties and interest on government bonds.

This made government bonds very popular. They sold well, as ordinary citizens could buy them in denominations as low as $50. But government bonds alone were not enough to restore the economy. The government printed more paper money: $450 million by early 1863.

To avoid inflation, meanwhile, the Internal Revenue Act of July 1862 taxed all incomes of more than $600 a year. It also imposed sales taxes on selected goods. The policy worked: At the end of the war, inflation in the Union was just 80 percent compared with 9,000 percent in the Confederacy. The North still saw industrial unrest, strikes, and riots as workers saw their real wages fall, but their hardships were nothing like those in the Confederacy.

At the U.S. arsenal in Watertown, Massachusetts, men work to fill cartridges with gunpowder.

A new economy

The North's financial policies changed the national economy forever. But with a national currency regulated by the government and a stable industrial base, the Union could pay for the war. It cost the North about $2.3 billion, or the equivalent of 70 percent of the 1859 gross national product.

1862 April–June

CIVIL WAR

APRIL 6–7, TENNESSEE In the Battle of Shiloh Ulysses S. Grant narrowly defeats Confederate forces, with heavy losses on both sides.

APRIL 12, GEORGIA Union agent James Ambrose steals a Confederate train on the Western & Atlantic Railroad. He is captured and hanged.

APRIL 29, THE SOUTH The Confederacy passes a conscription act forcing men aged 18 to 50 to enlist in the army; many farms go into decline as farmers join up.

APRIL 29, LOUISIANA The Union occupation of New Orleans opens access to the rest of Louisiana and the Mississippi Valley.

OTHER EVENTS

APRIL 8 UNITED STATES Inventor John D. Lynde patents the first aerosol spray.

April

The war created opportunities for profit for some industries, while others suffered. Any war-related industry, such as weapons and gunpowder manufacture, prospered. The Lincoln government encouraged enterprise, especially now that it was free of the Southern-dominated Democrats. They had blocked moves that might benefit free labor at the expense of slavery.

The Homestead Act of 1862, which offered settlers 160 acres of free land in the West, gave a major push to western migration. The Morrill Land Grant College Act meanwhile gave each state land to establish colleges to train farmers and mechanics, and it was the origin of many universities. The Pacific Railroad Act helped create a national economy that stretched across the country.

Some Northerners continued to live prosperous lives and to spend freely in stores.

Economic revolution

The Union's wartime economy created what has been called a "blueprint for modern America." It allowed the North to prosper during wartime and helped shift the economy from an agricultural base to a manufacturing base. The Republican Party also emerged as a long-term political power, with a commitment to industrialization and business that would mark the United States' future.

PROFITING FROM WAR

During the war certain products were in great demand, which allowed a few manufacturers to make huge fortunes. The Union war effort relied on private companies as well as federal arsenals and shipyards. The shipping tycoon Cornelius Vanderbilt, for example, built railroads during the war and became the richest man in the world. Wartime also allowed some prewar inventions to make their inventors rich. Gail Borden (1801–1874) had patented the process to make condensed milk in 1856. Canned condensed milk became an essential part of the diets of Union soldiers during the war, and Borden made a fortune.

MAY 31, VIRGINIA
The Battle of Fair Oaks (Seven Pines) is drawn. Union losses are 5,050 and Confederate losses are 6,150.

JUNE 1, VIRGINIA
General Robert E. Lee takes command of the Army of Northern Virginia after General Joseph Johnston is wounded.

JUNE 12, VIRGINIA
J.E.B. Stuart and 1,200 cavalry raid the Union camp outside Richmond, taking 165 prisoners.

JUNE 25, VIRGINIA
The first battle of the Seven Days' Campaign—the Battle of Oak Grove—sees McClellan's Union forces halted near Richmond.

MAY 5, MEXICO
A Mexican army defeats an invading French force in the Battle of Puebla.

MAY 20, UNITED STATES
The Homestead Act makes millions of acres of Western land available to settlers.

May   June

Foreign Relations in the Confederacy

Confederate foreign policy was the exact opposite of that of the Union. Southerners believed that the Confederacy's best chance of survival was to get European powers involved in the war.

This Union cartoon shows Confederate President Jefferson Davis trying to sell war bonds in Europe.

The Confederacy wanted other countries to acknowledge that it was an independent, self-governing nation. It also hoped that Britain's powerful Royal Navy would help break the Union blockade that stopped ships sailing into or out of Southern ports.

1862
July–September

CIVIL WAR

JULY 1, WASHINGTON, D.C. The Union introduces an Internal Revenue Act, imposing a tax on income to raise money to pay for the war.

JULY 13, WASHINGTON, D.C. President Lincoln reads a draft of the Emancipation Proclamation to his cabinet.

JULY 17, THE NORTH The Confiscation Act and Militia Act come into force, opening the way for the creation of black regiments of freed slaves.

AUGUST 29, VIRGINIA The Second Battle of Bull Run (Manassas) begins.

OTHER EVENTS

JULY 4, GREAT BRITAIN Lewis Carroll makes up the story that will become *Alice in Wonderland* to amuse a young friend.

JULY 14, UNITED STATES Congress introduces the Medal of Honor for valor in the military services.

July

August

The power of cotton

At the start of the war, the Confederate government hoped that Britain would take its side in order to preserve its cotton trade. By the start of the war, Britain had the largest textile manufacturing industry in the world—and the South was the world's biggest source of cotton. British Prime Minister Lord Palmerston and his foreign secretary, Lord John Russell, seemed to be on the Confederates' side. Referring to British cotton workers, they said they could not allow "millions of our people to perish to please the Northern states."

Confederate diplomats arrived in London in May 1861. They thought they had a good case to win British support. Their confidence grew when the British government declared that it would not take sides. It recognized the Confederacy as a belligerent power, which meant that the British believed the South had a right to go to war. Most of Europe followed Britain's lead.

The Confederate optimism was shortlived, however. The British government was determined to avoid a confrontation with the Union. Palmerston was a wily politician; he was determined to stay out of the conflict.

James M. Mason of Virginia was the Confederate envoy to Great Britain, but he had no official status.

A self-made problem

The Confederate tactic when dealing with Britain was to rely on "King Cotton." They placed an embargo on cotton exports. They thought that the need of British factories for Southern

---

AUGUST 30, VIRGINIA
Confederate Robert E. Lee defeats the Union army at Bull Run. His casualties stand at 9,500, while Union losses are 14,500.

SEPTEMBER 17, MARYLAND
The Battle of Antietam ends in a draw after heavy losses on both sides: Lee's Army of Northern Virginia suffers 10,000 casualties; the Union Army of the Potomac loses 12,400 dead, wounded, or missing.

SEPTEMBER 22, WASHINGTON, D.C.
Lincoln issues a preliminary Emancipation Proclamation.

SEPTEMBER 24, TENNESSEE
Union General William Sherman orders the destruction of every house in Randolph in revenge for Confederate shelling of his steamboats.

AUGUST 18, UNITED STATES An uprising by young Sioux Indians in Minnesota leaves more than 800 white settlers dead.

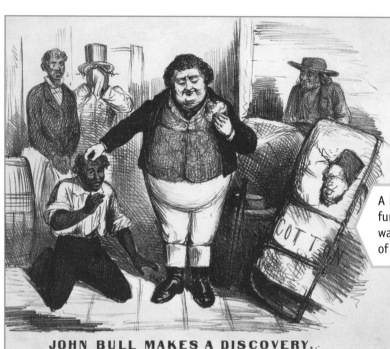

JOHN BULL MAKES A DISCOVERY.

A Union cartoon pokes fun at John Bull, who was a popular symbol of England.

cotton would force Britain to support them. In fact, Britain and France had enough cotton to last two years. By 1862, when they were beginning to run short of raw cotton, the Union had blockaded Southern ports, so the cotton could not be exported. Under international law, it was illegal to break a successful blockade. To get the British to break the blockade, the Confederacy would also have to admit that it had been holding back cotton. The British would not give in to such commercial blackmail.

BELLIGERENT STATUS

Belligerent status helped the South. In international law, it meant that the Confederacy was allowed to raise loans and buy arms abroad. But recognition as a belligerent status was not the same as recognition as an independent nation, which was what the South really wanted.

Confederate failure

The two main Confederate diplomats were James Mason in London and John Slidell in Paris. As late as September 1862 they still expected their mission to succeed. They thought that Europe's countries would recognize the Confederacy. The South had won a series of military victories that summer. They hoped that General Robert E. Lee's invasion of the North would make it clear that the South would win the war—and that Britain and France would then declare their support.

In the end, though, Confederate foreign policy was undone by events on the battlefield. Lee's failure at the Battle of Antietam (Sharpsburg) on September 17, 1862, changed the

1862
October–December

CIVIL WAR

OCTOBER 3, MISSISSIPPI
A Union army defeats the Confederates in the Battle of Corinth.

OCTOBER 11, VIRGINIA
The Confederate Congress passes an unpopular draft law that exempts anyone owning more than 20 slaves—the wealthiest part of society—from military service.

NOVEMBER 7, WASHINGTON, D.C.
Lincoln fires George B. McClellan as commander of the Army of the Potomac and appoints Ambrose E. Burnside in his place.

OTHER EVENTS

OCTOBER 8, PRUSSIA Otto von Bismarck becomes minister-president of Prussia; he uses his position to mastermind the unification of Germany.

NOVEMBER 4, UNITED STATES
Richard Gatling patents the machine gun that is named for him: the Gatling gun.

October · November

course of events. Victory at Antietam gave President Abraham Lincoln the opportunity he had been waiting for to issue his preliminary Emancipation Proclamation. Lincoln said that all slaves in the South would be free from January 1, 1863.

No one in Britain or France had any support for the institution of slavery. The British were particularly proud of having outlawed slavery across their huge empire in 1834. They had used their navy to help stop the African slave trade. By making the war a fight to end slavery, Lincoln had made sure that European opinion would support the Union and not the South. The South's original claim that it was fighting for the right to secede from the Union, and the North's stance that the Union must be preserved at all costs, were no longer the major arguments behind the war.

After Lincoln's Emancipation Proclamation, public opinion in Europe turned against the slaveholding South. Further defeats for Lee at Gettysburg and Vicksburg in 1863 meant that Confederate diplomatic efforts were ultimately hopeless.

The British-built CSS *Florida* is captured by the USS *Wachusett* in 1864.

A CONFEDERATE SHIP BROKER

In 1861 James D. Bulloch became an agent for the Confederate navy. He worked secretly in England to find shipbuilders to supply the South. This was illegal, because Britain's neutrality laws forbade building ships for a country involved in a war. Bulloch used smart ways to go ahead without technically breaking the law. By 1862 he had shipped two Liverpool-built cruisers: the *Florida* and the *Alabama*. The *Florida* destroyed 38 Union merchant vessels and the *Alabama* almost 80. After the war, Bulloch stayed in England. He was a wanted man in the United States. The U.S. government took legal action against the British.

DECEMBER 7, TENNESSEE
Confederates defeat Union troops at the Battle of Hartsville, opening up parts of western Tennessee and Kentucky.

DECEMBER 13–14, VIRGINIA
Burnside is beaten back in the Battle of Fredericksburg, with the loss of 6,500 Union troops.

DECEMBER 31, TENNESSEE
Union troops triumph in the Battle of Murfreesboro, taking Kentucky and increasing their hold on Tennessee.

DECEMBER 30, UNITED STATES
Lincoln reads his Emancipation Proclamation to his cabinet for comments.

DECEMBER 31, UNITED STATES
Lincoln signs an act admitting West Virginia to the Union.

Foreign Relations in the Union

The Union's foreign policy had one purpose: to get the rest of
the world to see the Southern secessionists as illegal rebels and
not as legitimate citizens of a new nation.

In this cartoon, Uncle Sam reminds John Bull of the British decision not to interfere in the war.

The Union government believed it was vital to persuade
European countries that the Confederacy was not an
independent country. The most important country to have on its
side was Britain, because of its economic power and the strength

1863
January–March

CIVIL WAR

JANUARY 1, WASHINGTON, D.C.
The Emancipation Proclamation
comes into effect, ruling that
slaves in the South are free. The
Civil War is now a war for the
abolition of slavery, as well as a
struggle to preserve the Union.

JANUARY 20–22, VIRGINIA
The Union Army of the
Potomac tries to cross the
Rappahannock River but turn
back as rain turns the ground
to mud.

OTHER EVENTS

JANUARY 1, UNITED STATES
The Homestead Act comes into
law, encouraging western migration
by granting land to farmers.

JANUARY 10, GREAT BRITAIN
The world's first underground
railroad line opens in London.

FEBRUARY 3, UNITED STATES
Newspaper editor Samuel Clemens
first uses the pen name by which
he will become famous: Mark Twain.

January   February

of its Royal Navy. Initial discussions went badly, however. The Union's secretary of state, William H. Seward, was aggressive when he warned the British that the Union would not tolerate any support for the South. The two most influential British politicians, Prime Minister Lord Palmerston and his foreign secretary Lord John Russell, did not like being threatened by Seward. They did not trust him.

Recognition or not?

From the start of the war, President Abraham Lincoln said the Confederates were rebels. He wanted to ensure that under international law the Confederates could not gain status as a belligerent power. That would mean the South had a right to fight a war. But Lincoln himself actually gave the South that status. At the same time as he demanded European neutrality, he declared a blockade of the Confederate coast. In legal terms, Europe could only be neutral if the war had two sides, and a country could hardly blockade its own ports. Therefore, the Confederacy clearly had a right to wage war. On May 13, 1861, Queen Victoria announced that Britain would remain neutral and recognize the Confederacy as belligerent. Other European nations followed Britain's lead.

The Confederates were delighted to be granted a higher status than that of a rebel state. The Confederacy could now

Secretary of State William H. Seward—third from right—hosts foreign guests at a garden party in New York State in August 1863.

MARCH 3, WASHINGTON, D.C.
The Union introduces the National Conscription Act, obliging men to join the army or pay $300 to hire a substitute.

MARCH 3, THE SOUTH
The Confederacy introduces an unpopular Impressment Act that allows army officers to take food from farmers at set rates.

FEBRUARY 24, UNITED STATES
Arizona is organized as a territory of the United States.

MARCH 3, UNITED STATES
The territory of Idaho is created.

March

A KEY ARCHITECT OF VICTORY

Charles Francis Adams (1807–1886) was the son of U.S. President John Quincy Adams and the grandson of President John Adams. As the Union's envoy to Great Britain throughout the Civil War, he proved a highly skilled and successful diplomat who defused many awkward situations. His manner contrasted with the abrasiveness of Secretary of State William H. Seward. Adams was well respected in London for his diplomatic skills.

Charles Francis Adams worked hard to ensure that the South did not gain British support.

lawfully raise foreign loans, buy weapons from neutral suppliers, and purchase armed vessels for sea patrols. Politicians in the South assumed that full recognition as an independent country would soon follow.

Seward was furious when he learned of the British decision. He ordered the U.S. envoy in London, Charles Francis Adams, to break off diplomatic relations with Britain if the British held any more meetings with the Southern envoys. Adams had arrived in England on the day of the Queen's announcement. He was more diplomatic than Seward in how he spoke to the British. Russell agreed not to receive the Southern envoys again, but he said that Britain would continue to recognize the South's belligerent status.

Strained relations

At the end of 1861, relations between Britain and the Union became so strained that they almost led to war. A Union sloop stopped the British ship *Trent* at sea and arrested two Confederate diplomats traveling on board. The action was illegal under international law. The British were furious. It was only the diplomatic skills of Adams, and the release of the Confederate diplomats, that managed to defuse the crisis.

The summer of 1862 saw relations become even worse. Although it had declared itself neutral, Britain was not stopping British merchant ships from running the Union blockade of Confederate ports. Shipyards in the British port

1863
April–June

CIVIL WAR

APRIL 2, VIRGINIA "Bread riots" break out in the Confederacy over the high price of food; the worst riots are in Richmond.

APRIL 17, MISSISSIPPI Union cavalry raids Mississippi, tearing up railroad lines. Soldiers ride south to the Union city of Baton Rouge, Louisiana.

MAY 2–4, VIRGINIA The Confederate Army of Northern Virginia defeats the Union Army of the Potomac at the Battle of Chancellorsville; however, Confederate commander "Stonewall" Jackson is shot by one of his own men and dies.

MAY 14, MISSISSIPPI Union troops capture Jackson, the fourth state capital to fall to Union troops.

OTHER EVENTS

MAY 22, UNITED STATES The War Department establishes the Bureau of Colored Troops.

April

May

of Liverpool were busy building armed cruisers for the South. Also, the British were beginning to think the Confederates might win the war after their victory at the Second Battle of Bull Run (Manassas) in August 1862. No European country would make an enemy of the Confederacy if it were on the point of victory.

In fall 1862 Emperor Napoleon III of France, who sympathized with the South, proposed that European powers help negotiate an end to the war. Britain supported the idea. The Union refused, however, because it would have meant recognizing the South as a separate nation.

Union success

Events on the battlefields in late 1862 turned the war in the Union's favor. When Lincoln's Emancipation Proclamation committed the Union to ending slavery, the Union cause took on a moral bias.

More Union victories in summer 1863 ensured that the British policy of "wait and see" would not lead to recognizing the Confederacy. Union foreign policy had succeeded. No matter how strained relations had grown across the Atlantic, Europe had stayed out of the war.

The *San Jacinto* intercepts the *Trent* in November 1861.

WAR WITH GREAT BRITAIN?

In November 1861 Captain Charles Wilkes of the Union sloop *San Jacinto* intercepted the Europe-bound British steamer *Trent*. The Union ship seized two Confederate diplomats, James M. Mason and John Slidell. News of their capture was celebrated in the North. But Wilkes's action broke international law. The British angrily demanded an apology and the release of the diplomats. As the extent of British fury became clear, the Union government started to worry. It even seemed that the British might go to war over the issue. In the end, common sense prevailed. The Union apologized and released the two diplomats.

MAY 18, MISSISSIPPI
Union armies begin the siege of Vicksburg.

JUNE 9, VIRGINIA
The Battle of Brandy Station ends in a Confederate victory.

JUNE 14, VIRGINIA
The Battle of Winchester is another Confederate victory.

JUNE 16, VIRGINIA
Lee orders the Army of Northern Virginia across the Potomac River to invade the North for a second time.

JUNE 28, WASHINGTON, D.C.
Lincoln replaces General Joseph Hooker as commander of the Army of the Potomac with General George Meade, whom he hopes will be more aggressive.

JUNE 7, MEXICO French troops capture Mexico City; the French want to begin a colony while Americans are distracted by the war.

JUNE 20, UNITED STATES
West Virginia is admitted to the Union following a presidential proclamation.

June

Government of the Confederacy

The Confederate government came into existence to
fight the war—but the administration of President
Jefferson Davis found the task almost impossible.

The Confederate
Convention met at
Montgomery, Alabama,
the first capital of the
Confederacy.

On February 4, 1861, representatives from seven states—
Alabama, Florida, Georgia, Louisana, Mississippi, South
Carolina, and Texas—met at Montgomery, Alabama. They
gathered to create a new nation. Speed was vital, because it

1863 July–September

CIVIL WAR

JULY 1–3, PENNSYLVANIA
The Battle of Gettysburg
yields 20,000 casualties
on each side in a
decisive Union victory
that marks a turning
point in the war.

JULY 4, MISSISSIPPI
The fall of Vicksburg
to the Union splits the
Confederacy in two.

JULY 13, NEW YORK
Antidraft riots erupt
across the North; in the
worst, in New York City,
African Americans are
attacked and draft
offices burned.

JULY 18, SOUTH CAROLINA
The 54th Massachusetts
Volunteer Infantry, a
black Union unit, fails
in a courageous attack
on Fort Wagner.

OTHER EVENTS

JULY 1, SOUTH AMERICA
The Dutch abolish slavery
in their colony of Suriname.

JULY, CAMBODIA French writers
reveal for the first time the existence
of the remarkable ruined city of
Angkor in the Cambodian jungle.

July

was clear to the delegates that war was close. They were also anxious to win support from the slave-holding states of the Upper South, near the border with the North, which had not yet left the Union.

On February 18, Jefferson Davis was declared the first president of the Confederate States of America.

A new start

The Convention came up with a constitution for the new country, but it did not clarify how power would be split between its federal government and its states. Slavery would remain legal in the new Confederacy but not the foreign slave trade, which had also been illegal in the United States. Reintroducing the slave trade would alienate Britain, which bought most Southern cotton. It would also annoy the Upper South, which wanted to protect its own trade in exporting slaves to the Deep South.

The choice of Davis as president was a smart compromise. With a distinguished military past, the planter from Mississippi was tall and elegant, like a traditional Southern gentleman. As a leading Southern Democrat, Davis had stood up for Southern rights. He supported secession but had a reputation for moderation. Such a balanced approach would make him acceptable to the rest of the world.

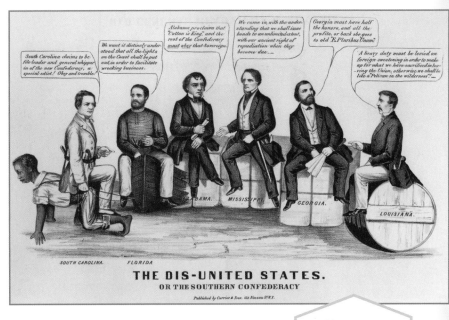

In this cartoon from January 1861, leaders of six states of the Deep South each sit on a symbol of the source of their state's wealth.

AUGUST 17, SOUTH CAROLINA Union forces begin a bombardment of Fort Sumter in Charleston Harbor, the place where the first shots of the war were fired.

AUGUST 20, KANSAS William Quantrill's Confederate guerrillas attack Lawrence, killing more than 150 civilians and destroying 200 buildings.

SEPTEMBER 19–20, TENNESSEE Confederates win a hollow victory at the two-day Battle of Chickamauga, losing 18,000 to the Union's 16,000, and forcing only a partial Union withdrawal to Chattanooga.

SEPTEMBER 29, ITALY Troops led by the nationalist Giuseppe Garibaldi defeat a papal army, a major obstruction to Italian unification.

A NEW CONSTITUTION?

The Confederate constitution echoed the U.S. Constitution of 1787. The Confederacy wanted to be seen to follow the principles of the Founders, so it tried to balance states' rights with federal power. The need to protect the rights of the states was the basis of the South's secession from the Union. In the South, each state was "sovereign and independent" but also part of a government. The states could not secede from the Confederacy as they had just done from the United States. A presidency could last six years, but a president could only serve one term.

Going to war

In February 1861, Davis sent a peace mission to Washington. Meanwhile, however, he was preparing for the war most Americans believed was coming. When Union warships tried to resupply Fort Sumter in South Carolina in April, Davis ordered the fort's bombing. The Civil War had begun.

Davis and his cabinet try to escape into exile after the surrender of the Confederacy in 1865.

Almost at once, Virginia, North Carolina, Tennessee, and Arkansas joined the Confederacy. Delaware, Maryland, Kentucky, and Missouri—all slave states— decided to stay in the Union.

Davis ran the war from the new Confederate capital, Richmond, the state capital of Virginia. Early military successes increased Southern optimism and the administration's popularity. Davis was elected unopposed as president in November 1861.

Unpopular measures

By the spring of 1862, any Confederate optimism was over. The Union armies had far more men, weapons, and supplies. They could attack on every front, while the Southern army was too small to defend its long borders. The number of Confederate volunteers had fallen off dramatically. Davis stunned the Confederate congress by asking it to pass a law to make all able-bodied men, between ages 18 and 35, serve in the

1863 October–December

CIVIL WAR

OCTOBER 15, SOUTH CAROLINA
Confederate submarine *H.L. Hunley* sinks on its second test voyage, drowning all its crew.

NOVEMBER 19, PENNSYLVANIA
Lincoln makes his famous "Gettysburg Address" during the dedication of the cemetery on the battlefield.

OTHER EVENTS

OCTOBER 3, UNITED STATES
President Abraham Lincoln proclaims the last Thursday in November as Thanksgiving Day.

OCTOBER 23, SWITZERLAND
The first conference of the International Committee of the Red Cross is held.

NOVEMBER 23, UNITED STATES
A patent is granted to the first process for color photography.

October   November

Confederate forces for at least three years. In April 1862 the Confederacy introduced the first draft law ever in America. This form of conscription was widely hated, however, because it was seen as unfair. Federal or state officials did not have to serve, and wealthy men could buy their way out by hiring a substitute. Davis also introduced martial law to deal with civilian unrest and imposed taxes to pay for the war effort.

Such moves increased the power of central government, which had been the cause of secession in the first place. But while Davis had many powerful political opponents—including his own vice-president—they were not united enough to threaten his position.

End of the war

The government then empowered the army to seize food and slaves for the war effort. But by the fall of 1864 the Confederacy was facing defeat. Davis decided his last chance was to free and arm slaves to fight. He forced the unpopular bill through Congress, but events made it irrelevant. On April 9, 1865, Robert E. Lee surrendered the Army of Northern Virginia. Davis fled but was caught a month later in Georgia.

This 1864 poster shows the most powerful men in the Confederate government.

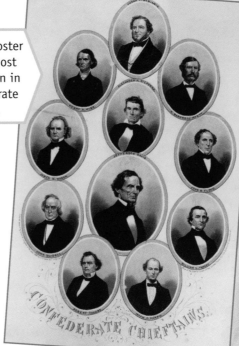

THE CONFEDERATE CABINET

Speed was of the essence when Jefferson Davis chose his first cabinet. He made sure that all the original Confederate states were represented. Robert Toombs of Georgia (a presidential candidate) became secretary of state; Christopher G. Memminger of South Carolina was secretary of the treasury. Leroy Pope Walker, from Alabama, was made secretary of war. Davis used the power given to the Confederate president to appoint ministers for political rather than practical reasons. Fourteen ministers served in the Confederate cabinet: six were imprisoned after the war, four were never arrested, and four fled the country.

NOVEMBER 23, TENNESSEE
The Battle of Chattanooga sees Union troops push back the Confederates.

NOVEMBER 24–25, TENNESSEE The Union capture of Chattanooga opens the "Gateway to the South."

DECEMBER 1, WASHINGTON, D.C.
Confederate spy Belle Boyd is freed from prison by Union authorities.

DECEMBER 9, TENNESSEE
After a 16-day siege, Confederate defenders withdraw from the town of Knoxville.

DECEMBER 16, TENNESSEE General Joseph Johnston takes command of the Confederate Army of Tennessee, replacing General William Hardee.

NOVEMBER 26, UNITED STATES
The first modern Thanksgiving Day is celebrated in the North.

DECEMBER 1, CHILE
A fire in a church causes panic in which 1,500 worshipers die.

Government of the Union

Although the federal government retained the basis laid down in the U.S. Constitution, it gained new powers during the war that would have been unimaginable before the conflict began.

The Thirteenth Amendment is finally approved after the end of the Civil War, in December 1865.

Abraham Lincoln realized when the war began that dealing with the conflict would require a major increase in the powers of both the government and of himself as president. He used his power in inventive and bold ways to help the Union.

1864 January–March

CIVIL WAR

JANUARY 14, GEORGIA Union General William T. Sherman begins his infamous March through the South.

JANUARY 17, TENNESSEE At the Battle of Dandridge, Confederate forces repel Union troops from the Dandridge area.

FEBRUARY 9, VIRGINIA A total of 109 Union prisoners escape through a tunnel at Libby Prison in Richmond.

FEBRUARY 14–20, MISSISSIPPI In the Battle of Meridian, William T. Sherman leads a successful Union raid to destroy an important railroad junction.

OTHER EVENTS

FEBRUARY 1, DENMARK Prussian forces invade the Danish province of Schleswig, beginning the Second Schleswig War.

January   February

A show of power

Congress was not in session when the first shots of the war were fired in April 1861. It would not sit until July. That gave Lincoln the chance to issue an executive order, or presidential command. He ordered the initial recruitment of 75,000 volunteers to put down the rebellion. He then ordered a blockade of Southern ports, an increase in the army's size, and the recruitment of a further 42,000 volunteers.

Lincoln continued to be bold in his use of presidential power. The most famous of all his executive orders was the Emancipation Proclamation, which he issued in its preliminary form on September 22, 1862. It declared that all slaves in areas still under rebellion would be considered free from January 1, 1863. Lincoln was widely criticized for acting in a nondemocratic and dictatorial way. He said his actions were part of his duties as commander-in-chief of the armed forces.

This group portrait shows President Lincoln, sitting in the center, with his most senior naval and military commanders.

Role of Congress

With regard to most nonmilitary matters, Lincoln let Congress decide government policy. One of its most pressing problems was how to fund the war. Wars had traditionally been paid for by government borrowing, but by 1862 the U.S. government was broke. Treasury Secretary Salmon P. Chase and leaders of Congress knew that they needed to make changes, but they

FEBRUARY 20, FLORIDA
Many men of the 8th Regiment of United States Colored Troops are killed or injured in the Battle of Olustee near Jacksonville; Union forces retreat to the coast.

MARCH 2, THE NORTH
Lieutenant General Ulysees S. Grant is made commander of all the armies of the United States.

MARCH 25, KENTUCKY Confederate cavalry attack the city of Paducah on the Ohio River; they retreat the next day, having suffered many casualties.

MARCH 14, AFRICA British explorers Samuel and Florence Baker discover Lake Albert at the headwaters of the Nile River.

Justin S. Morrill gave his name to the Land-Grant College Act of 1862.

were reluctant to impose taxes on a population that was used to very low levels of taxation.

In 1862 and 1863 Congress authorized the Treasury to print $150 million of paper money. The Legal Tender acts raised the total amount of paper money in circulation to $431 million. Nicknamed "greenbacks" because they were printed with green ink, these new bills paid the Union armies and helped keep them supplied.

Further innovative financial acts included the July 1862 Internal Revenue Act, which brought in the first U.S. income tax. The National Banking Act of February 1863 created a system to regulate the amount of money in circulation. One of the cumulative effects of these new acts was to shift power away from the states toward the federal government.

Expansion in the West

Another program the Republicans were eager to introduce was the Homestead Act. Passed in May 1862, it offered 160 acres (65 ha) of government-owned land in the West to settlers who lived on and farmed the land for five years. Another program was the Morrill Land-Grant College Act. It set aside 25 million acres (10 million ha) of public land for the creation of state agricultural colleges. In the same week Lincoln signed the Morrill Act, Congress passed the Pacific Railroad Act. It

FEDERAL POWER

Lincoln and many other Republicans started their political lives as Whigs. The Whig Party championed more power for the federal government in economic affairs. During the war, the former Whigs passed many of their programs into law, as their opposition was now in the Confederacy.

1864 April–June

CIVIL WAR

APRIL 12, TENNESSEE Confederate troops massacre the Union garrison at Fort Pillow, killing 202 African Americans.

APRIL 17, GEORGIA Hungry citizens of Savannah stage bread riots over the lack of food.

MAY 3, VIRGINIA The Union Army of the Potomac starts to move south, crossing the difficult terrain of the Wilderness region.

OTHER EVENTS

APRIL 10, MEXICO The French proclaim Archuduke Maximilian of Austria to be emperor of Mexico.

APRIL 22, UNITED STATES Congress decides to print the phrase "In God We Trust" on U.S. coins.

MAY 9, NORTH SEA Austria and Denmark fight a naval battle at Heligoland during the Second Schleswig War.

April   May

opened up the West by granting railroad companies 64,000 acres (26,000 ha) of public land and $16,000 in federal loans for the construction of a railroad to the Pacific Ocean.

Building for the future

As the war neared its end, the Union government had to help hundreds of thousands of former slaves cope with freedom. Most of these so-called freedmen were homeless, penniless, and illiterate. Congress set up the Freedmen's Bureau in March 1865. Its role was to help former slaves in whatever way it could: by reuniting families; setting up schools, colleges, and a court system; and helping freedmen draw up labor contracts with their employers. Although its funding was inadequate, the bureau did help many freedmen in the first five years after the war. It was the first example in U.S. history of a federal social welfare system.

Today, how much of a part federal government plays in daily life still divides the opinion of many Americans. Most historians agree that the Civil War created some of the building blocks of today's modern federal government. The smart use of federal power was a key factor in the Union's eventual victory.

A family of former slaves visits a Freedmen's Bureau in 1867 to get help from the government.

THE BIRTH OF CIVIL RIGHTS

The only change to the U.S. Constitution in the Civil War era came with the ending of slavery. Lincoln's 1863 Emancipation Proclamation did not actually free the slaves. That happened with the Thirteenth Amendment to the Constitution, in December 1865. In 1868 the Fourteenth Amendment was approved. It guaranteed citizenship to blacks. The Fifteenth Amendment of 1870 gave black Americans the right to vote. But another century would pass before the Civil Rights movement forced the nation to actually enforce the new amendments in practice.

MAY 5–6, VIRGINIA
Grant and Lee fight the inconclusive Battle of the Wilderness.

MAY 12, VIRGINIA
Grant and Lee fight again at the Battle of Spotsylvania. The battle is drawn.

JUNE 3, VIRGINIA
The Battle of Cold Harbor is a disaster for the Union army. They lose 7,000 men for no gain against Confederate losses of 1,500.

JUNE 27, GEORGIA
The Battle of Kennesaw Mountain sees Sherman's Union troops suffer heavy losses of 3,000 against Johnston's Confederate losses of 552.

MAY, GREAT BRITAIN
Charles Dickens publishes the first part of *Our Mutual Friend*.

MAY 26, UNITED STATES
Congress creates the territory of Montana, with its original capital at Virginia City.

JUNE 15, UNITED STATES Secretary of War Edwin M. Stanton creates Arlington National Cemetery, Virginia, on land previously owned by Confederate General Robert E. Lee.

Politics in the Confederacy

The biggest difference between Confederate and Union politics was the absence of political parties in the South. Some thought this an advantage, but many others were critical of Confederate policies.

The Confederacy's provisional congress meets for the first time in February 1861.

W hen the states of the Deep South seceded in February, 1861, delegates unanimously chose Democrat Jefferson Davis of Mississippi, a war hero, a seasoned politician, and a United States senator, as the first Confederate president. The

1864 July–September

CIVIL WAR

JULY 9, MARYLAND Confederates defeat Union troops at the Battle of Monocacy.

JULY 11, WASHINGTON, D.C. Facing strong Union defenses, Confederates withdraw from their attack on the Union capital.

JULY 22, GEORGIA Confederate General Hood's troops fail to defeat General Sherman's men at the Battle of Atlanta. Confederate losses are 8,000; Union losses are 3,600.

AUGUST 5, ALABAMA Union warships defeat Confederate vessels at the Battle of Mobile Bay. Union admiral David G. Farragut is said to have ordered, "Damn the torpedoes; full speed ahead!"

OTHER EVENTS

JULY 5, UNITED STATES The Bank of California is founded with holdings of $2 million.

JULY 14, UNITED STATES Gold is discovered in Montana at Helena, which will later become the state capital.

AUGUST 8, SWITZERLAND The first Geneva Convention is held to discuss the treatment of wounded soldiers in war.

July   August

vice president was a Whig, Georgia's Alexander H. Stephens. When elections were held in November 1861, Davis and Stephens were elected unopposed.

By mid-1862, the war was going badly for the South. The government's popularity fell after Davis passed a number of unpopular laws, particularly the Conscription Act in April and the "Twenty-Negro Law" in October, which allowed plantation owners to avoid the draft. Adding to the administration's difficulties, inflation was destroying the Confederate economy.

Davis's popularity plunged, and he almost lost control of the Senate in the congressional elections of November 1863. Much of the criticism centered on Davis himself, who could seem cold and uncaring.

A powerful opposition

One of Davis's harshest critics was Vice President Stephens, who constantly attacked the president. State governors meanwhile criticized Davis for taking away "states' rights," the principle on which the Confederacy had been founded. The South had outlawed political parties, however, so there was no single opposition for Davis to take on—and no loyal party to back him.

By 1865, Confederate politics, just like the war, were collapsing. Confederate citizens no longer supported their Congress. By the time the war was finally lost, most Southerners paid tribute to the bravery of their fighting men, but few had any good words for the political leaders they felt had let down the Confederate cause.

The front page of a Union magazine reports the election of Jefferson Davis as the Confederate president.

AUGUST 31, ILLINOIS The Democratic National Convention in Chicago nominates General George B. McClellan as its presidential candidate on an antiwar ticket.

SEPTEMBER 1, GEORGIA General Sherman cuts the last supply line to Atlanta, the railroad, forcing the Confederates to leave the city.

SEPTEMBER 16, VIRGINIA Confederate cavalrymen raid Union beef supplies on the James River to feed hungry Southerners.

SEPTEMBER 22, VIRGINIA Union forces defeat Confederates at the Battle of Fisher's Hill and start to destroy crops in the Shenandoah Valley.

SEPTEMBER 5, JAPAN British, Dutch, and French fleets attack Japan to open the Shimonoseki Straits to navigation.

SEPTEMBER 15, ITALY The new country gives up its claims to Rome; the Italians agree to make Florence their capital.

September

Politics in the Union

Along with its superiority on the battlefield, the Union was able to defeat the Confederacy because it had a sound political strategy and a visionary leader in Abraham Lincoln.

Lincoln reads the Emancipation Proclamation to his cabinet in September 1862. The members held a range of views on slavery.

At the start of the war, the Republican Party of President Abraham Lincoln had been in existence for just seven years. The party was a loose collection of people with different opinions; Lincoln's task was somehow to hold them all together.

1864 October–November

CIVIL WAR

OCTOBER 19, VIRGINIA
Union forces, under General Sheridan, defeat General Early's Confederate Army of the Valley at the Battle of Cedar Creek.

OCTOBER 26, ALABAMA
Union forces at Decatur prevent Confederates led by John Bell Hood from crossing the Tennessee River in an attempt to cut William T. Sherman's lines of communication.

OCTOBER 27, VIRGINIA
Union forces assaulting the Confederate capital at Richmond are defeated in the Battle of Fair Oaks.

OTHER EVENTS

OCTOBER 11, UNITED STATES
Slavery is abolished in Maryland.

OCTOBER 30, AUSTRIA The Peace of Vienna ends the Second Schleswig War between Germany and Denmark.

OCTOBER 31, UNITED STATES
Nevada is admitted to the Union as the 36th state.

October

The majority of the Republicans, like Lincoln, had formerly been members of the Whig Party, from which the Republican Party had evolved. A significant minority, however, had once been Democrats. Although slavery was a a major cause of the war, Republicans had a wide range of opinions about it. A few, known as Radical Republicans, wanted an immediate end to all slavery. A larger minority were Free Soilers, who tolerated slavery where it already existed, but were opposed to its spreading into new western territories.

Following the secession of the Confederate states, the Republican Party had large majorities in both houses of the U.S. Congress. This enabled it to pass several important laws, including the Homestead Act (1862), the Morrill Act (1862), and the Pacific Railroad Act (1862).

The opposition

Lincoln recognized that, to govern effectively, he needed the support of the opposition Democratic Party. But by 1862, the Democrats had split into two factions. The War Democrats supported the war effort, but the Peace Democrats, or "Copperheads," wanted a negotiated end to the war. Lincoln appointed many War Democrats to high offices and military commands. Using his presidential powers, on the other hand, he cracked down hard on Copperhead leaders and their activities.

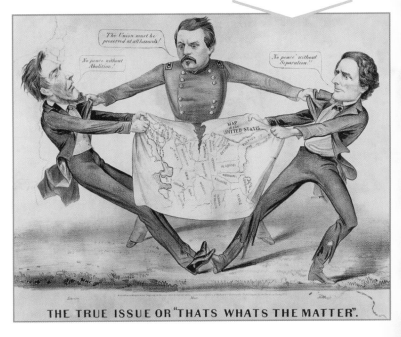

This 1864 cartoon shows Democratic hopeful McClellan looking on as the two presidents rip the nation apart.

THE TRUE ISSUE OR "THATS WHATS THE MATTER".

NOVEMBER 4, TENNESSEE
Confederate cavalry commander Nathan B. Forrest completes a 23-day raid in Georgia and Tennessee by destroying a Union supply base at Johsonville.

NOVEMBER 15, GEORGIA
Union general William T. Sherman burns much of Atlanta before setting out on his notorious "March to the Sea."

NOVEMBER 25, NEW YORK
Confederate spies fail in a plot to burn down New York City.

NOVEMBER 8, UNITED STATES
Abraham Lincoln is reelected for a second term as president of the United States.

NOVEMBER 29, UNITED STATES
Militia in Colorado massacre some 200 Cheyenne and Arapaho at Sand Creek in retaliation for an attack on settlers.

LINCOLN'S CABINET

Lincoln picked his cabinet to represent a cross-section of Northern political views. Secretary of state William H. Seward was a former Whig who was often critical of Lincoln. Democratic members included Navy Secretary Gideon Welles and the war secretaries Simon Cameron and Edwin Stanton.

An 1864 campaign banner for Lincoln and his running mate, Andrew Johnson.

After Lincoln announced his preliminary Emancipation Proclamation in September 1862, he faced Congressional elections in the fall. The Peace Democrats fought a concerted campaign against the government. They gained 35 seats in Congress, won control of the legislatures of Illinois and Indiana, and had governors elected in New York and New Jersey. Still, the Republicans kept overall control of both houses of Congress, as well as a majority of the state governments.

Consolidating power

Lincoln faced growing opposition from within his party, however. Radicals wanted him to free slaves in Union territory without delay and enlist them in the army. The Radical Republicans controlled the Committee on the Conduct of the War. They used the committee to investigate Lincoln's handling of the conflict and criticize the administration.

Lincoln's opponents saw the 1864 presidential elections as an opportunity to change the course of the war. Lincoln used his political skill to outmaneuver them. First, he forced the resignation of his own treasury secretary, Salmon P. Chase, who was popular with the Radical Republicans. Then Lincoln strengthened his power base by making sure that his supporters controlled the Republican national convention,

1864–1865
December–January

CIVIL WAR

DECEMBER 13, GEORGIA
Union troops capture Fort McAllister near Savannah.

DECEMBER 15, TENNESSEE
At the Battle of Nashville, the Confederate Army of Tennessee is defeated by the Union Army of the Cumberland.

DECEMBER 20, GEORGIA
The Confederate garrison escapes from Savannah.

DECEMBER 21, GEORGIA
Sherman and his men enter Savannah unopposed at the conclusion of the "March to the Sea."

OTHER EVENTS

DECEMBER 8, VATICAN Pope Pius IX publishes the Syllabus of Errors, which condemns liberalism and reformism.

December

which met in Baltimore in June. Lincoln removed his vice president, Hannibal Hamlin of Maine, to make way for Andrew Johnson, a Tennessee War Democrat. To boost the party's appeal, the Republicans also temporarily changed their name to the National Union Party.

The Democrats nominated the popular Union General George B. McClellan as their presidential candidate, but Lincoln's victory was overwhelming. He carried all but three states and won 55 percent of the popular vote.

Post-war reconstruction

Lincoln's popularity was at its peak after the 1864 election. The Union was close to winning the war, and thoughts turned to what would happen after the conflict. Lincoln came up with a moderate plan for Reconstruction. When he was assassinated in April 1865, the Radical Republicans in Congress opposed a similar plan proposed by the new president, Andrew Johnson. Instead they passed the 1867 Reconstruction Acts, which gave African Americans the right to vote. The measure was highly unpopular, however. Once Reconstruction was overthrown in the mid-1870s, black Americans were once again denied civil rights.

Benjamin Wade was a leading Radical Republican.

FIGHT FOR RECONSTRUCTION

Lincoln's plan for Reconstruction in the South was too lenient for the Radical Republicans. In July 1864, Benjamin Wade and Henry Winter Davis proposed the Wade–Davis Bill. It did not give African Americans the right to vote, but it would force white Southerners to take the "Ironclad Oath." They had to swear that they had never shown disloyalty to the Union or supported the Confederacy, otherwise they would not be able to vote or hold office. Although the bill was passed by Congress, Lincoln refused to sign it into law. He believed that punishing the South would do more harm than good.

JANUARY 15, NORTH CAROLINA
Wilmington, the last port in Confederate hands, is closed.

JANUARY 19, SOUTH CAROLINA
General Sherman vows to march through the Carolinas.

JANUARY 31, VIRGINIA
Robert E. Lee is named general-in-chief of all the Confederate armies.

JANUARY 4, UNITED STATES
The New York Stock Exchange opens its first permanent headquarters.

JANUARY 27, PERU
Peru's independence is established in a treaty with Spain.

JANUARY 31, UNITED STATES The House of Representatives approves an amendment to the Constitution abolishing slavery; it will become the Thirteenth Amendment.

Republican Party

The Republican Party was just seven years old when the Civil War started. With its inspirational leader, Abraham Lincoln, the party steered the Union to victory and set the course of post-war recovery.

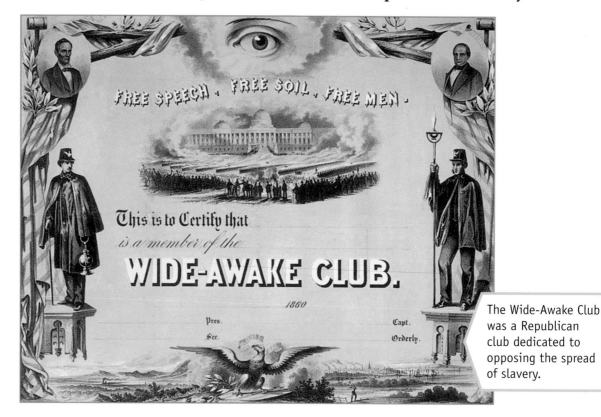

The Wide-Awake Club was a Republican club dedicated to opposing the spread of slavery.

T he Republican Party had only been formed in 1854 during the political crisis over slavery that would lead unavoidably to the Civil War. It began to govern on the eve of the conflict, and was still in power during the Reconstruction period.

1865
February–March

CIVIL WAR

FEBRUARY 3, VIRGINIA
President Lincoln and Confederate representatives fail to agree a diplomatic ending to the war.

FEBRUARY 16, SOUTH CAROLINA
Columbia surrenders to General Sherman's Union troops.

FEBRUARY 17, SOUTH CAROLINA
As Union troops enter Columbia, someone sets fire to cotton bales. Over half of the city is destroyed in a huge blaze.

FEBRUARY 27, KENTUCKY
Confederate guerrilla leader William C. Quantrill and his band attack civilians in Hickman.

OTHER EVENTS

FEBRUARY 12, UNITED STATES
Henry Highland Garnet becomes the first African American to speak in the House of Representatives.

FEBRUARY 22, UNITED STATES
Tennessee adopts a new state constitution that outlaws slavery.

February

A new party is born

The Republican Party came into being when a group of politicians opposed to slavery began to meet in 1854. They had previously belonged to the Whig and Democratic parties but were united by their opposition to the Kansas–Nebraska Act. The act had repealed the 1820 Missouri Compromise, which had effectively forbidden any expansion of slavery in Northern territories.

Within only two years the Republicans were organized enough to contest the 1856 presidential election. Their candidate for president was John C. Frémont, a well-known military leader and explorer. Frémont ran under the slogan "Free Soil, Free Labor, Free Speech, Free Men, Frémont." Although he lost to Democrat James Buchanan, he won a significant 33 percent of the popular vote.

By the time of the next presidential election in 1860, the Whig Party had split up, the Democrats were divided about slavery, and the Republicans were growing stronger. Their candidate, Abraham Lincoln, was elected and became the first Republican president. His election led to seven Southern slave states seceding from the Union.

"God and Our Union" was a song published in 1860 to support the Republican cause.

A program of change

Southern politicians, who were all Democrats, left the North— and left the Republicans without an effective opposition. With huge majorities in both Houses, Lincoln's party was able to

MARCH 2, VIRGINIA
The Shenandoah Valley is in Union control after the Confederates lose the Battle of Waynesboro.

MARCH 3, WASHINGTON, D.C. The U.S. Congress sets up the Freedmen's Bureau to help deal with the problems resulting from the sudden freeing of tens of thousands of slaves.

MARCH 13, RICHMOND
The Confederate Congress passes a law authorizing the use of black troops.

MARCH 19, NORTH CAROLINA
Joseph E. Johnston attempts to stop the march of Union general William T. Sherman through the Carolinas in the Battle of Bentonville; he is defeated late the following day.

MARCH 4, UNITED STATES
Abraham Lincoln is inaugurated for his second term as president.

MARCH 18, SOUTH AMERICA
Paraguay goes to war with the Triple Alliance of Brazil, Argentina, and Uruguay.

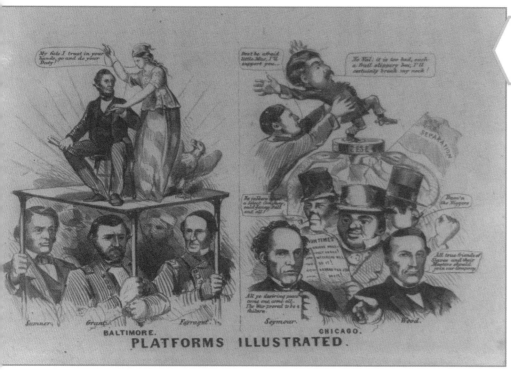

This Republican cartoon of 1864 mocks the Democrats for wanting to make peace with the South.

introduce new economic programs to promote free labor and enterprise, including the Morrill Land-Grant College Act of 1862 and the Homestead Act of 1862. The Republicans also introduced higher tariffs on imports. This helped to protect U.S. firms by making imports more expensive, and it raised money to pay for a transcontinental railroad.

The Republican Congress was also able to rush through legislation to pay for the war. It introduced a federal income tax and printed paper currency, known as greenbacks, to pay for the armies.

CRUSADE AGAINST SLAVERY

For the highly vocal Radical Republicans, the Civil War was about the need to abolish slavery and to punish the South for its behavior. Never a majority, the Radicals still managed to dominate the more moderate elements of the Republican Party.

Divided party

Despite the Republicans' congressional majorities, Lincoln had a difficult job holding the party together in the first year of the war. The Union suffered a number of military setbacks, and Republicans were divided on slavery. The so-called Radical Republicans argued that the emancipation of slaves should be a Union war aim. Conservative Republicans wanted a gradual

1865 April–May

CIVIL WAR

APRIL 1, VIRGINIA
The Battle of Five Forks ends in defeat for the Confederate Army of Northern Virginia.

APRIL 2, VIRGINIA
Grant attacks Petersburg and the Confederates start a retreat from Petersburg and Richmond.

APRIL 6, VIRGINIA
Lee loses 8,000 men to Union attacks at the Battle of Sayler's Creek.

APRIL 7, VIRGINIA
Grant asks Lee for his army's surrender; Lee asks for terms.

APRIL 9, VIRGINIA
Lee surrenders to Ulysses S. Grant at Appomattox Courthouse.

OTHER EVENTS

April

emancipation, which slave states would undertake voluntarily. Lincoln did not join either camp, but he soon became convinced of the need to use emancipation as a weapon in the war. In September 1862 he issued his preliminary Emancipation Proclamation. It declared that all slaves in the rebel states would be free as of January 1863. Lincoln had transformed Republican war aims from a political determination to preserve the Union to a moral struggle for human freedom.

A call to patriotism

As Union victory became inevitable, Republicans argued that Lincoln's reelection in the 1864 presidential election was more a question of patriotism than a party issue. They temporarily changed their name to the National Union Party and produced a pamphlet called "No Party Now But All For Our Country." Lincoln chose a Democrat, Andrew Johnson, as his running mate. They easily won the election.

The assassination of Lincoln soon afterward left his party without a leader but in a powerful position. The Republicans had saved the nation.

This cartoon from the election campaign of 1864 shows Lincoln being upended by the issue of emancipation.

A REPUBLICAN SUMMER

The Civil War began a remarkable period of Republican dominance. From Lincoln's election in 1861 until President Herbert Hoover left office in 1933, 72 years later, a Republican was president for all but 16 years. The Republicans' longevity owed much to progressive acts such as the Homestead Act of 1862. The farming communities of the West created by the act became Republican heartland. Republican politicians were also quick to remind voters that they had saved the nation in the Civil War. This tactic—sometimes called "waving the bloody shirt"—remained powerful well into the 20th century.

APRIL 14, WASHINGTON, D.C.
President Lincoln is shot while watching a play at the theater.

APRIL 15, WASHINGTON, D.C.
Lincoln dies from his injuries; Vice-President Andrew Johnson becomes president.

APRIL 26, NORTH CAROLINA
Confederate General Joseph E. Johnston surrenders to General William T. Sherman.

MAY 10, GEORGIA
Confederate President Jefferson Davis is captured and taken into custody.

MAY 29, WASHINGTON, D.C.
President Andrew Johnson grants an amnesty and pardon to Confederate soldiers who will take an oath of allegiance to the Constitution.

APRIL 21, UNITED STATES
Lincoln's funeral train leaves Washington, D.C.; Lincoln's body is carried in a Pullman sleeping car.

APRIL 27, UNITED STATES 2,000 Union soldiers aboard the riverboat Sultana die when it catches fire and sinks on the Mississippi River in Tennessee.

MAY 1, UNITED STATES
Walt Whitman publishes "Drum Taps," his long poem about the Civil War.

NEED TO KNOW

Some of the subjects covered in this book feature in many state curricula. These are topics you should understand.

People:
Abraham Lincoln
Jefferson Davis
Clement Vallandigham
George B. McClellan

Confederacy:
Draft laws
Foreign policy
Political opposition
States' rights

Union:
Democratic factions
Economic reform
Presidential powers
Republican Party

KNOW THIS

This section summarizes three major themes of this book: the economics of the war, foreign affairs, and politics in the North and South.

ECONOMICS

FISCAL REVOLUTION
The Union funded the war by printing paper money and raising taxes; the South adopted similar measures, which were highly unpopular with Southerners opposed to the idea of central goverment.

INFLATION
Both the North and the South suffered inflation, or rising prices. In the South, however, a combination of printing more money and a shortage of goods led to ruinous inflation rates of 9,000 percent.

FOREIGN AFFAIRS

RECOGNITION
The Confederacy was desperate to be recognized as an independent nation. Thanks to skillful Union diplomacy, however, the leading European countries instead decided to remain neutral.

EMANCIPATION
Once Lincoln's Emancipation Proclamation of 1862 made the war a struggle to free the slaves, the South lost any chance that any major power would recognize its independence.

POLITICS

- Both Abraham Lincoln in the North and Jefferson Davis in the South were widely criticized for how they exercised their powers.
- Lincoln made unprecedented use of Executive Orders, which allowed the president to govern by decree.
- Political parties were banned in the South, which weakened opposition to Davis but also meant that he did not have one unified opponent who would be easier to take on.
- Because Southern Democrats withdrew from the U.S. government, the Republican Party was able to enact laws with little opposition; it remained the dominant party for over 70 years.
- Abraham Lincoln included War Democrats in his government and in the army, but he took harsh measures againsts Peace Democrats, who wanted to negotiate a treaty with the Confederacy.
- Lincoln was very worried that he would lose the presidential election in 1864, but Union successes on the battlefield put him in a strong position.

TEST YOURSELF

These questions will help you discover what you have learned from this book. Check the pages listed in the answers below.

1. **How did the Peace Democrats get their nickname of "Copperheads"?**

2. **Why did Southerners believe that "Cotton is king"?**

3. **How high was inflation in the Confederacy by the end of the war?**

4. **How much of the country's wealth was produced by the North?**

5. **What was the purpose of the Homestead Act of 1862?**

6. **Which diplomat represented the Union government in London?**

7. **Where was the first capital of the Confederacy?**

8. **What was Abraham Lincoln's most famous executive order?**

9. **Why wasn't Lincoln's moderate plan for Reconstruction put into practice?**

10. **What was the Republican Party's temporary name in 1864?**

ANSWERS

1. After a poisonous snake (see page 9). 2. Because the South provided three-quarters of the world's cotton (see page 11). 3. 9,000 percent (see page 13). 4. Three-quarters (see page 15). 5. To encourage migration to the West (see page 17). 6. Charles Francis Adams (see page 24). 7. Montgomery, Alabama (see page 26). 8. The Emancipation Proclamation (see page 31). 9. Lincoln was assassinated before it could happen (see page 39). 10. The National Union Party (see page 43).

GLOSSARY

abolition The ending of slavery; supporters of abolition were known as abolitionists

belligerent A country that is legally involved in a war

blockade Measures aimed at preventing trade by using ships to intercept vessels heading toward port

cabinet A group of politicians who advise the President

Confederacy A league of members united by a common purpose; the word was used to describe the Southern side in the Civil War

convention An assembly that meets to discuss what political ideas to follow

Copperheads Democrats in the North who believed the Union should make peace with the Confederacy

dictator A politician who governs on his or her own, without consulting the government

diplomacy Relations between countries

emancipation Another word for "freedom"

federal A word referring to the U.S. government in Washington, D.C.

inflation A general rise in prices

infrastructure The basic facilities of a country, such as roads or ports

martial law A system in which the army is responsible for law and order

neutrality A position in which a country does not take sides in a war

plantation A large-scale agricultural estate; in the South, plantations were used to grow crops such as sugar, tobacco, cotton, and rice

planter Someone who owns a plantation

radical Someone who holds extreme views

secession Breaking away from the Union; states that seceded from the Union formed the Confederacy

tariffs Taxes placed on imported goods

Union The United States of America; the word described the Northern side in the Civil War

FURTHER READING

BOOKS

Baxter, Roberta. *The Northern Home Front of the Civil War* (Why We Fought: The Civil War). Heinemann Library, 2011.

Baxter, Roberta. *The Southern Home Front of the Civil War* (Why We Fought: The Civil War). Heinemann Library, 2011.

Koestler-Grack, Rachel A. *Abraham Lincoln* (Leaders of the Civil War Era). Chelsea House Publishers, 2009.

Krensky, Stephen. *The Emancipation Proclamation* (Documents of Freedom). Marshall Cavendish Benchmark, 2012.

McNeese, Tim. *Civil War Leaders* (Civil War: A Nation Divided). Chelsea House Publishers, 2009.

Mountjoy, Shane. *Causes of the Civil War: The Differences Between the North and South* (Civil War: A Nation Divided). Chelsea House Publishers, 2009.

Stanchak, John E. *Eyewitness Civil War*. Dorling Kindersley, 2000.

Wagner, Heather Lehr. *The Outbreak of the Civil War: A Nation Tears Apart* (Milestones in American History). Chelsea House Publications, 2009.

Williams, Jean Kinney. *Jefferson Davis: President of the Confederacy* (Signature Lives). Compass Point Books, 2005.

WEBSITES

www.civilwar.com
Comprehensive privately run, moderated site on the Civil War

www.civil-war.net
Collection of images, written sources, and other material about the Civil War

www.historyplace.com/civilwar
The History Place Civil War timeline

www.pbs.org/civilwar
PBS site supporting the Ken Burns film *The Civil War*

www.civilwar.si.edu
The Smithsonian Institution's Civil War collections, with many primary sources

INDEX